This book may not be reproduced in whole or in part, except in the case of reviews, without permission from

Wildheart Press
P.O. Box 1115
Jamaica Plain, MA 02130.

Cover image: Arrival copyright ©2001 by Lynne Mendes
Interior design and production: letta neely

The text of this book is set in Baker Signet.
The cover font is American Typewriter.

.

First edition.

Library of Congress Cataloging in Publication Data
Neely, Letta, 1971-
    here: poetry/by letta neely

ISBN 0-9663097-5-8

here.

poetry by letta neely

Contents

Contents

*Dedicated
to
Seana Murphy*

because this whole earth is ours

we must be intimate magic
when obituaries
read like a roll call
of our neighborhoods

It is not enough to mention names to know locations of
to know locations of past iniquities
of present torture
when we are called
to remove our feet from
cacophony's piss; to dance away every lie
that refrains movement

it is not enough to raise stylish fists in cut-throat air
to pontificate eloquent tragedies over coffee and croissants

we must
pick sharp shards of bloody souls
from bloody pavement and caress them correctly

we are called to suture particular
pieces of memory now

we must drape ourselves
n dream through death n hunger
now only for liberation from oppression
which teaches of borderland geographies
where even imaginations are restricted, shown
barbed-wire fences
and trenches of murdered comrades

we are called now to use crazy magic words
to cast spells; to pull knives
from back pockets
from behind teeth; we
are called to push over bronze statues
of dead anglos on horses; to defy the boxing in,
the chaining up,
any definitions which hold and creep like viruses inside

we are called to know the power of language
to make love the only recipe of our desire
to cure in ways of our elders

we must hack off
each finger wrapped tight n desirable
around our arms, yanking us to complacency

we must do down-home jigaboos
plant words found in no dictionary
bathe each other with soft freedom
when the order of things threatens to numb possibility

we must sing long ass wordless wails
right there on sidewalks
when we feel small and packageable

we must let them see our anger up close

for our tongues know songs
to bring raindrops
when they teach us these dry white seasons

and

everything we give our energy to
is prayer

Later.

Of what her eardrums ate with a disinterested stare, my father's
Spittle swollen with hate, jackhammered into her heart's beat was a
reason.

He could say "fuck you, bitch" masterfully, precise as a surgeon
in the stolen organs business.

She walked around feeling empy. Her horn stuck on
muffled tones,
this new bird didn't caw so much. She tried to follow the recipe

exactly. She wasn't free to range
\\\\\\\\\\\

exactly.

Now these days, that madman cancer runs
Stark naked

Through my father, digs his claws
Into daddy's precious

He didn't go to the doctor until
His pimp got too affected.

Nevermind he couldn't see
One ear can't get no sound

Nevermind. His walk got
Fucked up so he went to the doctor.

I got one theory say that cancer is an amazon stalker
Coming down his highways at a fast pace

Seeking sultry revenge and my mother's organs back.

Precise in her laughter.
Precise in her roar.

I got another story that yells at the top of its lungs;
"daddy, don't go yet" while shadows of him skinnier
than his hunger move in long lines going anyway

Daddy

My father was born in east st. louis
next to arch of bluesville
being black and therefore poor and
therefore often hungry
for more than food
he went to jail often

a jail is not different than east st. louis
in 1936 when blackmen
could be picked up for whistling too loudly
on street corners
or bashed in the head for looking (maybe
probably not)
at a white woman

there are still standing pyramids
of knowledge lost in him
Blackman standing 6'2" now always
crouched over finding solace
in a 40oz

time is running on and
soon no one will remember
that my father was an incredible artist
on paper, in the kitchen, and in
the infinite times he began remodeling
the house
no one will remember that he skatted to
jazz early Sunday mornings
when our world
was quiet

no one will remember

and they would dismiss
him as
the drunk
spread out in front of the tv
snoring

another random flashback

cacophonous
starts while walking this time   i see a little girl
in the car with an older man and
earth shifts underneath me and i drop my cigarette,
see this 12 year old me hovering above
asking me to hurry up, come get her

i stand at the border, stretching for her hand, we
barely touch and when his hands grab her
she sizzles and sounds like a little girl crushed
between two semis-- that cracking is her pelvic
bone, she will have hip problems her whole life--
her breath is escaping into silence
i try to catch it with my hands
stockpile it
for other impending emergencies.

explanation or at the threshold of my life.

lately/ I write/ these poems/with all/ these slashes./ please/ understand/
lately/ this is what my life looks like/ oil covered fields/
cement skies/ scarce space left /raggedy /around /bullet//
holes// obituaries// dry blood/ are in the air/ and I who am
in awe of air/ am caught/ in/ betwee/n the molecules/ oxy-
gen is stuck in cellophane//
hydro//gen is on the other side ////shuffling and suffocating.
u see/
I want/ my breath back/ all of it. I want inhale and exhale to
mean
something/ but I find whole days have fallen out of my body
like lost keys though a hole I tore in my pocket so I could
masturbate in the library. I know the orgasm of life but
cannot get in my house.

. u see/ I walked/ from hell// u see my baby brother died//
u see I thought I had loved this whole place with my whole
heart// n my baby brother died/ the same
way// they// make/ some colored boys// leave.// gun n
regret in another colored boy's hand.// I grew up on this,
ya'll./ n I loved this place anyway.// // but loss ain't/
ain't a word the dictionary holds// I cain't find// ramon// no
mo/ that was not him lowered in to the ground/ / I knew a
blk boy who ran from fights once./ who yelled for his big
sister n brother// to come kick ass/ I didn't know

this man who carried a gun/ whose nickname
was monster// I knew this blk boy who remembered every-
thing he heard down to timbre of voice. / I knew this boy/
who lost/ his first friend at age 9//// u see/ I tell u/ he
used to juggle oranges in the living room.//and I miss the
way he manipulated air so precise n casual

11

I thought/ I knew murder//

chiapas/ byrd/ shephard/ picket/ kosovo/ diallo/ workfare/

all made me ancient moan./ I was an observer

murder slices insidious lies on my wrists.
I have been fighting gravity to get back here.
the whole trip is a minefield/
/ I have lost/ limbs to come back here/

I lost my key. n (oh lawd) I hide whenever anybody
answers the door.

first anniversary of my brother's death

the day before my father left
he took them all to dinner
and then shadow boxed on the patio
his bare hands built
he threw his cigarettes in the trash
and willed us the rest of the world
he woke up really only once
in the hospital room
sat up straight in bed at midnight
his skin sagging arms in the air
shouting " I won, I won"
and we who had not been sleeping
laughed and celebrated the good fight
and then he was gone again
soon for good

July 4rth

firecrackerbaby boy/ blew your nose all down
your face when you were little/ one time/ u drew
a picture of a cracked wine glass and a little boy/
u wrote stop the drinking in red crayon/ teach gave
you an a+/ I found it in the children's art file of the filing
cabinet/ abandoned since mommy left daddy/ came home
for your homegoing/ they say you said the lord's prayer with
somebody's mama before you died in the alley three blocks
from our house/ for the life of me/ I have imagined too
much bloodless of you for this to be real/ the finality/ the
end of my preparations/and false anticipations of your
death/ when it is final: the other edge of rope we'd been
holding dangles unprecarious
dangerous

from the kosovar poems

wonder where
there is to go
for rest when
everywhere is
a battleground
a bloody ground
an accidental target
when there are no
accidents. don't wonder
how it is to be caught
in crossfire since
here I am ducking
bullets in America
too. shuffling from
place to displacement
hoping not to be confirmed
in my grief.

I want
muscle flexing this sad
anger to confirm I am
alive fighting. it is
summer and at night
my lover and I lie
on the futon in the
front room guessing if the
sounds are cars backfiring
internal gunfire or bombs

Mona and Lisa on a greyhound bus

Nobody knew what came over them.
it was a long trip but all of
this was uncalled for. Or maybe the sweet smell
of Lisa's snatch did call
Mona's nose to nuzzle; then teeth
to nibble. It was a long ride

they both wanted to enjoy it and they did.
Fuck the lady who kept turning
her head in disbelief,
holding up her magazine
And peeking over.

At first, Mona was just laying
her head in Lisa's lap--
her thick thighs a perfect
place to nap---
but Lisa's fingernails
Trailed Mona's back—on top of
then under her shirt,
a swirl and down, her fingers mapping (laying)
out the desires she had---
she'd scratch
A little line then
gloss soft touching tips of back hair,
down on the spine, over the sides of Mona's body
then down again--- right near the ass bone---
but not quite.

Mona played like she was deeply sleep—acted like she was
hibernating—all the while
enjoying Lisa's touch,
but she did turn her head so her cheeks nuzzled right between

Lisa's thighs and when she inhaled
she got wet and dove/
> Fuck the kids that walked by to the restroom,
> Fuck the guy in the seat behind them---they all
heard Lisa catch her breath, it
escaped like a not so subtle scream and
She pushed herself onto Mona's face.

Mona put her fingers as far into Lisa's pussy as she
could with Lisa's pants still on---
but Lisa was drenched and fabric gives
and she didn't give a fuck if Mona made a hole—
Mona
made a hole big enough for her hand to burrow though,
then her tongue.

Mona thought the bus driver might stop the bus:

Pull over,
kick them off, make them walk back to boston unsatiated
but she couldn't help it—

she couldn't stop to care
what might happen

it was the "dream"
come true;

public
moving sex in front of

all kinds of people and
their smells, and church's chicken,

and grunts mixing with distorted blaring radio headphones
and hamburgers and movie of godzilla in background
and het couple in the backseat next to the bathroom
doing the same thing they were doing

Don't rock the bus, don't
Rock the bus baby,
        Lisa sang in a low voice
        As she rocked mona's hand, mona's face

Are you my boy, baby? She asked,
Yeah, are you my bitch.

Lisa rocked her pussy on mona's tongue
        She rocked her pussy on mona's tongue
        Mona's tongue rocked lisa's pussy
        When Lisa came the lady
        Rattled her magazine so loud
        They thought she came too.

3 movements

        morning
harvesting your nectar
is my favorite
task
just dip down
until I taste
horizon on my
tongue
brilliant
as mumia's liberation

        noon
        (Short fisting hallejuah)
girl,
when you
come
I swear I
feel god
squeezing
my
hand

        night falling
over this city
in 3 shades of
blue. sky is
open as our legs
some nights/ I arch
my neck
let air sit
on my face

terror

talking to you on the phone is running a police gauntlet
and falling into cotton towels laced with fiberglass. as more we
become less idol to each other, I think about denouncing my
citizenship to your country. not the whole mother land, just the
earthspace where we lived together in fear's dungeons,
polishing our bars for fun.

Mone, 1975-1998

what map written for the four of us can be valid for now 3?
all signs, roads, modes of travel shift meaning from here on
out.
The difference drastic as 4 gunshots to the back.
All roads blocked. Traffic backed up and stacked along the
entire length of my intestines. Moving less than 2 miles an
hour; carbon dioxide—the extent of breath.
No other exits offered.
No slippery when wet roads.
Just stalled with the heavy stench of road-killed deer
carcass splattered over the highway. You were. You were such a
Graceful-eyed boy.   This is how deep and how bloody
we will pause our speech,
Our tongues maneuver with weary grace as we remember not
to include your name among the living.   The headlights
Will make us freeze to the oncoming traffic.

Attention: Lesbians at Funeral

pictures are quiet and subtle in their finality
our irises do expand and contract into already cropped
versions of certain universes.

we see what the taker wanted us to see—
sometimes more or less

amongst this pile, there are photos of secret intimacies—
quick shared smiles of cousins,
a stolen kiss from my pregnant sister to her boyfriend
even a private untameable moment between my parents—
divorced now for years—
a pretty reminder of how we got here

there are no pictures of my brother and his white wife
relaxing into their laughter

no pictures of you rubbing my forehead,
my head in your lap as I spin from tequila
that tasted like car oil that needs to be changed.

in the markings of this time, there is nothing
no reminder that says
we are each other's touchstone

no eyemagic caught on film
that will say to anyone after us
that we existed together

these are the things that tell me we are still not seen
that we are unwanted children of familial gatherings
these are things that transcend the niceties that made

you feel welcome in our house

they decide to refocus, avert yes, choke on pronouns
alter the whole
claim us as outskirts of frames, outcasts of blood,
render us outside of mourning

Here, I have developed pictures
of how you held me the afternoon
I was doubled over in my sorrow,
puking up the taste of my brother's death. you held
me like night holds
all the stars in the safe darkness
of her womb

this picture is patchwork, frayed at its edges,
worn-in,
comfortable

this picture cannot be taken

After walking down Newbury Street & Downtown Crossing

all the glittering attractions drag us like magnets
while insidious ones creep through sly as paper cuts
insidious as cavities.

deluge of commericals in every medium is torture.
old folks say too much of anything is bad for you.
we gorge on essences & generics & bootleg versions of everything.

we sharecrop our own bodies,
go down into the mines of ourselves for capitalism, come up
hacking, smiling
with new shirts made
in Indonesian sweatshops

tonight another person has been killed in codman square--
the news is interrupted by a "Diamonds are Forever" commerical
& I'm thinking blood diamonds on your ring fingers
can't bring nothing but bad luck
(like unwrapping an egyptian pharoah when you've been warned)

Cuz his mama can't buy him back to life with it.

Riding the F Train

riding the F train
in the only empty car
at 2pm on a Sunday
afternoon
as
an
open invitation
to fuck

as the train barrels
from one stop to another
a kiss lead to
another kiss leads to
you flat backed
on cold plastic seats
                    begging

The doors open—
our breath bated, bodies waiting to be sated—
we wait
no one; door shut tight again
ramble—lights flicker bright and dark

you on your back leads
to my hand underneath your shirt
unfastening

you unbuttoning my jeans
and my hand underneath your skirt—
            you're not wearing any underwear
                    "I know" you respond
            your wetness soaks me. You're
            coming down

rainstorm
already

Next stop 34th street

The train stops/ opens its gaping mouth
You shut your legs, I jump up
sit your back pack over my crotch

Again, no one enters the train

you snatch my jeans down
to my ankles

Open your legs again, sit
across the aisle legs spread wide
open

wet cunt smiling
some slick ass hungry smile

I put on my best look like a boy look
take my travel dick out my bag

let you wait for this

I watch you wait

                        watch you swallow your own fingers with your
pussy

                     "Don't". That's all I'm gonna say
                     It's a promise you take lightly as you suck
                     on drenched fingers;

switch hands,
reenter yourself , then

"Make me stop"

I lift you up, push your back against
emergency door
sit you down on this dick
you get comfortable,
you get insatiable

you gonna ride this
for all its worth

ride this ride

until we get caught or
come

apology

I never meant to love
More than you alone
But love entered and enters
All of my pores
From everywhere
Like a tentacled spectacle

Home (2)

here is where it is, baby I want to be here
Inside this sweet pussy playground you have got it
Rocking and wet on my leg, you like to be
Bossed around and I like to tell you to
Get on your hands and knees and take
It all, this whole love into you and sometimes
I am soft and gentle with my hand and fist and
tongue but then you push your pussy against
me like you really are addicted and will stop
at nothing to get what you need and this is what
I love about your body: your ass, how sweet you
taste, your pretty titties, your thighs & your neck,
your toes how they curl when I run fingers
down your back, nibble behind your knees
the way you squeeze my jawbones to displacement;
& sometimes when we are moving too fast u take me in your
here is where it is   on the edges & core
of here is where I want to be with you tasting
every nectar I crave and always craving more

steen fenrich.

I dream your skull all the time. now.
last night, I spent erasing black scribbles
of your social security number and the words
dead nigger faggot #1.
All. gone. All erased
from your pretty head.

Number One Cold War Asylum

The cold war had me shivering, clattering unborn dreams
making plans for dismissal should we ever be bombed

I could only imagine white girs in tanning booths, big hair and
sculpted-brown bodies sizzling inside out instantly, the blood
volcanic in its desire for exit; three-legged mangy dogs hobbling
down main street; babies poisoned by curdled breast milk;
mushroom clouds over albuquerque; the roaches,
who my father fought daily—having the last laugh

The governor transparent as clean water, his voice bursting like a
ripe mango, told us the production of ball bearing, little pieces of
steel, smaller than skittles, a little bigger than exploded
shrapnel make war work.
He said we were number one in the field.
Bombing us, he said, would put a cog in the union's wheel.

At school, there were drills once a week, after lunch. On our knees,
heads down. In cold and dingy hall.

There was one skinny brown boy who picked his nose an entire
drill, pasted them on the walls and floors, told everybody we would
be the first to go bye-bye.

The principal dragged him the afternoon he swallowed a bottle of
Nyquil between periods. His groan was rumbling though my
intestines for weeks. Stalking like how the governor described low
flying Russian bombers coming to get us. It is no wonder why
death and ballbearings have held my attention ever since,
why I shiver at the stalking unseen

my parents stocked up on canned goods and toothbrushes believ-
ing religiously in eternity

I was going to lay naked in the front yard. Spread my brown arms to sky. And wait.

[not Brandon   not Matthew   not Versace]

If you're not a primetime contestant
nobody cares if you don't
survive on this island

you could be dismembered, throat slashed in midtown manhattan,
left in a new mexican valley, gutted with knives in your own living
room,

you could have been running for your life or stalked. you could
have been working the streets or coming home from a restraurant.
when you were murdered.

one thing is for sure:
you are definitely brown
or black, indigenous or
immigrant, queer
& forgotton
by newspapers,
moviemakers,
& new scholarship funds

Doorways

yr fingers call me
home from exile
say if you want to dance,

On being an American going to Roxbury

A cabbie at fanueil hall
demanded money
upfront.
I replied "I know my rights, I'm
a civil rights lawyer, don't fuck
with me!"

He got out,
came over to my door,
yanked my arm through the window
since I had locked the door

I had money in my pocket. Telling you this now,
in case you decide already--like those tourists--
that I was broke and marring the landscape.

I was bleeding heavy and cramps were sitting in my gut
like racism and I was not getting out of that cab.

But none of those snobby white tourists were interested
they were standing at the cab stand gawking,
hands up to hail my cab. I was on the curb
soon. pissed.
embarrassed to be a yelling black bitch in public
I got up quick,
staring at these white motherfuckers
caught the train.

Now that america's twin talismans have melded skin and metal,
sank down to smouldering fire and asbestos in firemen's alveoli,
these same people want to say I am american (unhyphenated),

Pardon me for laughing

Water Sign

I falling in love with water
She swallow me whole, caress
me to my marrow, this woman
make my muscles tingle n stretch
into her wetness like blues sometime;
sometime like jessye norman voice or regina carter violin
this woman shake my foundation where it faulty
show me where she make a better standing ground
she dance whirlpools and tidals
she dance me into whole notes with her hands

Conversation with my Abdoulaye

"You know," he says in english
tilted pleasantly by his dark, uncompromising
senagalese accent, "how if you
have a full cup of water with dirt
on top. You know how it looks
muddy, not clear? The dirt--
it goes down to the bottom
of the cup settling there
if it sit long time."
He fingers his remaining dreads,
pulls from the pages of his journal the branches of his life
she cut from his head saying,
          "if you want to get a job
          here you have to be
          clean cut"
but "this is my hair", he tells me,
"I was in the place in my
life when all the water was
becoming clear and she take
me from my land, say she love
me, bring me here and then
she shake the cup and everything
was muddy again."

Afterbirth 2

A hole punched so far into infinity of home Bones
pitted of marrow; once mined
solemnly

the first tastes of my mother's milk—
beginnings of longings worth entrancing the unknown
world from womb;   this hole comes

in myriad ways first my mother betrayed
me. I didn't know it was foreshadowing
this deciduous

journey back many worlds from this—
I am trying to shed blame's baggage; to sew
truth's lineage stitch by stitch. Here.
I unpacked this to give you:

> You were
> my closest love,
> the first
> I craved
> to know was you

the rest: wood ants gnawing nuclei from molecules. paralysis
waltzes down my morale;
I have come to understand contradiction:
Sometimes i
paint myself with poisons
the city dump
refuses   and I glow in the dark.

I want to live.

I want to dive into the awesome wreckage
like a spelunker—
helmet light to avoid pitfalls, sudden bumps, stalactites.

The first room was all
In darkness and I recall loving you meant
I knew what you felt like inside. I want to remember

everything portal is
an entrance and an exit.

I have refused many
wombs, many umbilical cords,
darksightedness

unable to take the longing into this body

prayer while laying on tarmac, looking up

Stars, I need you
to open up
to preach your
secrets to me like a holy
rolling preacher.

something has to fall
down on me, fall down
on me, match this place
I am on the floor with something
that will raise me
to my self

Love poem for SUN

So there's this story inside me. right, it's got the beginning and the ending but no middle yet. that's you and me and then maybe if that's true, then maybe the story inside me is waiting for you so I can get on with my life. when you come around corner, baby, I swear it's always love at first sight. you don't take my breath, you quicken its pace and if you asked me I would abandon all the other loves to rise with you.

Nights, I sit waiting for you to come home, sipping tea and shivering as the gas oven on high is not your rival. do you remember how long we've loved each other, how you and I and sky are blood relations. the front yard tree and me nestled in crook of its arms, and the two of us fucked by your heat and sky's breeze. I've always loved in threes, eversince.

You are the shiny one, the one who makes me watch you walk in and out of my life every day. you love your grand exits and entrances more than even I do. you love what your body can do. all you do is fuck and make love and have sex all day. A nymphopyromaniac. but you cultivate relationships and you pull me back from my coldest spaces and you warm my feet and you brush your fire against my lips and you hold on and you pull back and you give the most unconditional love. period. everlasting.

Sometimes I risk losing my sight to stare at you

rope

rounded bitter bite
draped round neck

impostered bomb
burned into skin

history unfurled

for all his moans
they had the radio up loud

once they turned it down
on account of a whitemans' dare

to hear blk mans' moans

skin, the muscle, cartilage
and bone, the tongue, the open
throat, the brain drenched through
eye
all leave their sounds
cleaving air solo in reckless desperation like
rocks during tractor plow.

stalking nonbelievers and believers alike,
their sounds cut off breathing like
gravel impounded windpipes,

he was scraping mother
earth with his hair, then
head, then skull, then bits of bone
flying up in reckless desperation like rocks
during tractor plow.

Still Image #1 (rwanda, spring 1994)

arched entrance to red brick catholic church
jesus' white arms outstretched
beckoning

your eyes go down the stairs. your
        eyes go down the stairs. your eyes
            go down the stairs. your eyes go
                down the stairs. your eyes go down
                    the stairs .your eyes go down the
                        stairs .your eyes go down the stairs

        weeds frame her   blood is soaking her white shortsleeved
        shirt her black legs haphazard under her skirt. she died
        here. weeds whispered instructions for her journey. her
        arms and legs bruised, brown, outstretched
        and beckoning

Abdoulaye says

"If you have headache in senegal
everybody knows
you get a frog and you put
his belly on your
head, and he piss
and 5 minutes later
you never felt better
but, you know
sometimes
you are so sick, the headache is so strong
that, I don't know why
but the frog, he take everything
he make you well
but in five minutes that
frog, he is dead. So me, I say,
Ahm, gonna take aspirin"

oh god, legba, shango, obatala, mommy

I feel swollen, parched,
emaciated, scared, raw,
alone, numb, tight,
tight, in need of laughter,
I miss things I can't
hardly remember
my brother
somedays everything
I have left leaves
me hanging from
only my fear of falling
I am returned to guttural
languish of moaning,
internal dialogues in
strange tongues, I am
in need of interpret,
in need of my
spinebone being
salved

Dancing with the Ancestors

Black people do incomprehensible thangs in they bodies
Be like we never left home
Be like home gets reciped from air
in foot stomping and food stamps,
the way she twist her waist
pump her pelvis improvised
like dinner or heat in hungry people's houses

Our bodies congregate holy spaces,
Make each other cornerstones where
Conversation is a movement taking us
Into our joints' first, anxious and ancient breaths

We know we know our bodies
Unchained
Especially when we are dancing--
          slide
                    And slide and spin and step
          back and
                    twirl--

And it's a lot through
The bloodstream a drumbeat and somebody
In the kitchen puttin dey foot in the greens and
"Girl, even when everybody was on a different
Time---nobody missed a step."

Our series of movements is a storyteller
Make believing present tense from old hands
And asking spirits to twist
Configurations no geometry
Can predict

At parties, in cars, in our living room,
This soul train struts down birth canal,
Traces lineage like rivers
Rushing past dams of controlled flow

People be precocious as robins' eggs, black
People do incomprehensible thangs in they bodies

Legba and Oshun be laughing
Like snakes in a fresh skin as our
Heads be spinning on cardboard squares in church
Parking lots, feet raised up, kissed by same
Heat that kisses the motherland

The walls be laughing, the stove and sink too,
Even the refrigerator and microwave chuckle
Incense curls up into ancestors' nostrils; and
There are even those moments of mourning
Hugged up in the beads of perspiration and
Certain angles of dip and stretch.
And who's rocking who is uncertain
And unnecessary knowledge.

people get so drunk off
spirit, swear they see familiars.

Friday Nights

Mona nibbling neck in the restroom at the theatre.
Lisa didn't think she would make it
through dinner and a movie without coming.
Mona take her food into her mouth slow, she chew slow,
she smile when she chew. She take in every
taste, look up a Lisa. Swallow when
she ready. Smile again. Chew.

Some Friday nights, Lisa
don't wear no panties.
Some Fridays she like
it when Mona rip 'em off
and she got to search
the Sunday ad pagers
for lingerie sales. Some
Fridays, she put Mona's dick
and harness in her purse.
Tell Mona to hold her purse while
she go to the restroom. Tell Mona
her breath stank and to check in
there for some chewing gum or something.
Some Fridays, Lisa flirts with every butch
around while Mona watches. Some Fridays,
she let Mona dance with other femmes,
just so she can interrupt,
take her sweet daddy back
behind the coat rack,
give her something
special, 'fore they
get home.

Why lisa don't mind washing the floor

Early Saturday mornings
she rise when sun come
through slats of shades. First thang she do,
she turn look at her lover
curled, a conch shell hard
and soft as the nearest high tide.
Then she git up, wrap that ole
purple terrycloth robe round her nakedness,
put sarah vaughn on the turntable. She be thinkin
ain't a goddamn thing like sarah vaughn's voice
cept my mona's fingers playin
my body like bass notes held past
heavens. She thank god for
Friday nights.
Oooh child. She be on her
hands and on her knees, scrubbin the floor,
thinkin   is the water as a hot
as i have been?
She dunk that rag in the bucket.
Take both hands to wrang it out.
Still, water drips in warm spirals
down her wrists,
touches her elbows and it comes to her
redemption's deja-vu. Mona on her
knees, head down between lisa's thighs--
a fat honey bee gorging on nectar and
bringing it back to lisa's lips.
And she opened up to mona wide like evening
primroses to full moons,
LIke she visiting the sky full of constellations.
She member she praised mona's mama n
she praised mona's daddy for havin her,

she member she really thought they could make
a baby with this much love.
She member she couldn't even count how
many times she rose to a penultimate horizon
and the thangs she saw there.

Shiiiit, lisa be sniffin the floor as
she scrub it. She love smellin
aftersex much as she love
her bare back on kitchen floor.

some mornings

some
mornings
sweetness
dawns ebony hills
on either side of my face
i indulge deep red sky

Blues

we did something for you and you damaged us
we gave you be-bop n blues n moans n shouts n we gave you
hallelujah
n you gave us james byrd's wings broken and featherless
left us his dust ingrained
bone from the last drag
language must move his
final screams to our
throats

House of Fear

The house of fear has no windows and no
 doors,

the fourth graders tell me,

then how do you get out?

You put gasoline around the stove
And you turn on the gas

Then you climb out the chimney
And scream for help

Sometimes you have to
Break a leg or something   she said

Home (I)

After a years absence   you call
my name   again   I enter

your world timid   this time

I am unwrapped   devoid of costumes

shorn of lies   and   single.

you have a daughter now   a singing siren

of a child   who crawled u in your life like a sanctuary

I am standing   in your living room   permeated
by her heart beat   she jumps into   these arms
            and feels familiar

you say listen, do not come here too afraid to stay.